Poems for When You Can't Find the Words

Poems for When You Can't Find the Words

Edited by
Mary Shine Thompson

Gill Books

Gill Books
Hume Avenue
Park West
Dublin 12
www.gillbooks.ie

Gill Books is an imprint of M.H. Gill and Co.

Poems for When You Can't Find the Words initiated by Irish
Hospice Foundation in partnership with Poetry Ireland.

9780717193738

Designed by Bartek Janczak
Printed by CPI Group (UK) Ltd, Croydon CR0 4YY
This book is typeset in 10.5 on 16.5 Dolly Pro.

The paper used in this book comes from the wood pulp of
sustainably managed forests.

A CIP catalogue record for this book is available from the
British Library.

5 4 3 2 1

Contents

Part 2: Poems for carers and the bereaved

Foreword

'I have no words ... There are no words ...'.

'No words' was like a mantra when I recently, and suddenly, suffered a double bereavement. Everyone struggled with words, including me and my family, the bereaved.

Poets had words though, and we reached out to them in our pain and confusion. The words of Christina Rossetti at one funeral – 'Remember me when I am gone away, / Gone far away into the silent land; / When you can no more hold me by the hand, / Nor I half turn to go yet turning stay' – and W.B. Yeats's *Lullaby* recited at the graveside of the other.

The gift that poets share, and have shared over the ages, is the ability to find words when we have none. We are grateful to poets – all poets – but particularly the poets living and dead whose words grace this book. We thank them for the time spent without expectation of reward re-organising words upon a page until they reach an approximation of understanding. For articulating these huge, bewildering experiences that stretch the limits of human understanding. We thank all poets for accompanying us in our time of need.

We thank Mary Shine Thompson for the love and dedication she has shown in choosing the poems for this book.

Reading it I realise that the shadowlands of grief are time-less, that the sensations of loss are universal across the ages. This book offers the empathy and comfort of words shared by poets centuries ago.

We thank Poetry Ireland, especially Jane O'Hanlon and Niamh O'Donnell, as well as Creative Ireland, Dublin City University, and Gill Books, whose patience and support made this book possible. Finally, our thanks to the team at Irish Hospice Foundation led by CEO Sharon Foley, in particular Dominic Campbell, Lynn Murtagh, Rebecca Lloyd and Rebecca Kelly.

Irish Hospice Foundation holds space to reflect on death, dying and bereavement. To each of you reading this book, we hope you find one voice among all those gathered here which holds space for you. We hope this book gifts you some words.

Jean Callanan,
Chair of Irish Hospice Foundation

Introduction

Sometimes, 'words alone are certain good', as W.B. Yeats wrote. Good words can gladden the heart at the best of times, and they can enliven the misery of the worst of times. Sometimes, though, the right words in the right order remain tantalisingly beyond our reach: when, for example, emotions are raw, or formless, or just overwhelming. The more momentous an event, the greater the challenge to find the words for it.

The best words in the best order are, nonetheless, within reach: they may be found in verse. By enriching conventional language, poems can condense meanings and compress feelings. They can tone down background noise and see into the heart of things, illuminating aloneness. They can open up chinks of wonder even in the most troubled times.

Poetry has other strengths too: it is a portable and accommodating art, a companion as much at ease in a sick room or hospital ward as at the fireside. It speaks to the fears and concerns that illness and approaching death awaken. It brings dignity to a mysterious process which people have been pondering since time immemorial. It shares the wisdom gleaned from millennia of reflection. Poetry can keep us going.

The readers who were foremost in our minds while preparing the selection of poems in *Poems for When You Can't Find the Words*, are, in particular, you, the members of the Irish Hospice Foundation community: you who know that your passing is not beyond the blue hills, but around the next bend of the road. Probably you have been encouraged to 'put your affairs in order'. But the 'affairs' that deserve your attention go beyond legalities and documentation. They include affairs of the heart. This collection invites you to engage in conversation with the most elegant, skilled conversationalists on topics of crucial importance at this time. It also addresses a second circle of readers: your family, friends and carers – those who suffer loss and bereavement. In reality, all the members of the Hospice community will find some solace and pleasure in this selection of poems.

The team behind *Poems for When You Can't Find the Words* was clear about the kinds of poems we wanted to offer readers. They would echo Seamus Heaney's final message to his wife in the hours before he died: 'don't be afraid'; or, as he put it, 'noli timere'. The poems in this collection do not deny that gloom might encircle death and bereavement; but they all offer at least a flicker of light. They do not gloss over the lonely road ahead; instead, they 'give sorrow words'. As William Shakespeare observed, 'the grief that does not speak knits up the overwrought heart and bids it break'. Some of the poems in this anthology admit to anger and rage, yet they are not dominated by negativity. They infuse the deluge of emotions surrounding death with beauty; after all, as Francis Bacon said, 'the autumn of the beautiful is also beautiful'.

Readers will find short, accessible poems or brief excerpts from longer poems, mostly, but not exclusively, written in English since the mid-twentieth century. Many are by poets from, or associated with, Ireland. While some poems are familiar and well loved, the schoolroom does not dominate the selection. To encounter poems like Dorothy Duffy's 'My sister is not a statistic' or Brendan Kennelly's 'Begin', will hardly surprise. In the dark days of Covid-19-induced distress, they revived our drooping spirits.

This collection also contains fine verse sharing the experience of grief, love and loss that spans the barriers of time, geography and language. Some has survived millennia. I know that I belong to the same human race as the poet Sappho when I read Caitríona Ní Chleirchín's contemporary take on a two-thousand-year-old expression of love. I join with Anne Bradstreet, the seventeenth-century American poet, in celebrating her husband. I empathise with the anonymous medieval poet who rails against the tragic loss of a child, and I recognise the anxiety tormenting a fellow human being facing their final journey in 'Each day brings the same three talking points'. The pain of these anonymous poets forges an intimate bond across centuries in contemporary versions specially commissioned from Paul Muldoon.

Dual texts in Irish and English, some specially commissioned by Poetry Ireland, offer access to the wisdom and aesthetic of Irish-language verse. Alan Titley's prose poem in Irish and English, 'An Fear Dána', for example, re-imagines the anguish of a widower depicted in a thirteenth-century poem as if his wife died only yesterday. Another exciting feature of this anthology is the inclusion of specially commissioned poems by poets who are members of new and diverse communities and who bring fresh vigour to our sense of Irishness.

Readers will find poems on the loss of lovers, parents, siblings and friends, and heart-rending evocations of children's lives cut short. The focus is on the now; on quiet, intimate conversations rather than on long or declamatory public poems. 'There is only now', Vona Groake reminds us, a 'now' that is worthy of quiet celebration. Louise Glück's resilient 'Snowdrops' savours that momentous 'now'. And the fleeting present need not deprive readers of a sense of humour. Ciaran Carson's 'Fear' and John O'Leary's 'To-do List' will bring a wry smile to our dwindling days. Readers will welcome words that honour carers and the physical effort involved in caring; indeed, Seamus Heaney's poem 'Miracle' does just that. Some poems bind the personal with public tragedy, such as Eiléan Ní Chuileanáin's 'The Morandi Bridge'.

To read or hear these poems is to engage in conversation with trustworthy friends, the kind who avoid jargon and euphemism. Friends who know when to nod, hint or affirm; when to speak out candidly; and when to move on in silence. Don Paterson's poem 'Nil Nil' says it straight: 'this is where you get off, reader; / I'll continue alone'. The right poem shows an interest in your affairs, as a friend might. It doesn't presume to hold all, or even any, of the answers, but it creates a safe, cliché-free zone in which you can be at ease, and where the to-and-fro of a heart-to-heart might bring some peace and clarity. To facilitate relaxed exchanges, the poems are not arranged in a rigid structure. Rather, they raise and return to topics and create the kind of loose links that invite you, the reader, to participate in the conversation.

The power of words to spark change is nothing new to the Irish Hospice Foundation (IHF), whose remit is to provide end-of-life and bereavement care. Its team has long recognised the potential of poetry to complement and enhance its work. When the concept of producing a selection of verse for its community was mooted, it was natural that IHF would look to Poetry Ireland, the national association committed to achieving excellence in reading, writing and performing poetry. The two associations are natural allies. Their combined skills, complementary philosophies and mutual collaboration led to this collection.

The idea originated in a chance conversation between Dr Jane O'Hanlon, Poetry Ireland's education officer, and Rebecca Lloyd, the IHF's then public engagement officer, in 2020, just as the Covid-19 pandemic was changing lives irrevocably. They agreed that the Hospice community would benefit from the kind of honest words that are, as George Seferis says, 'strong enough to help'. Soon their enthusiasm attracted an informed, enthusiastic *meitheal* ready to respond.

Rebecca Lloyd, along with Rebecca Kelly, IHF's communications coordinator, and Lynn Murtagh, IHF's head of marketing and communications, shared the wisdom gleaned from their work with the Hospice. From late 2020, Dominic Campbell, the IHF's arts officer, coordinated efforts. The Poetry Ireland team lent the project its poetic sensibility and professionalism. Stalwarts included Niamh O'Donnell, Poetry Ireland's then director; Catherine Ann Cullen, the poet in residence at the time (2019–2021); Elizabeth Mohen, Poetry Ireland's programme officer; and Dr Jane O'Hanlon.

Dublin City University, through the office of its president, Professor Dáire Keogh, contributed seed funding, and support was also provided by the Creative Ireland Programme. Professor Máirín Nic Eoin advised on Irish-language poetry. Deirdre Nolan of Gill Books immediately recognised the anthology's potential. Rachael Kilduff, Deirdre's successor as editor, has been unfailing in her attention to detail and in her dedication to the anthology. My task was to select the poems and introduce the book.

The team that compiled *Poems for When You Can't Find the Words* fervently hopes that its poetry will be a perpetual star shedding light and candour on the Irish Hospice Foundation community, and far beyond.

Mary Shine Thompson

PART 1:
POEMS FOR PATIENTS

From SERENADE

GERALD DAWE

The still of evening —
a grey evening, it has to be said —
slates of the house
beyond have loosened,

a slate-grey pigeon luffs by
and from the kitchen
the washing machine's final cycle spins
faster and faster like so many lives.

There is only now
to toss around
like a small word
in an empty box,
a single, low-slung
rain cloud
gaining on
the bay.

LATE FRAGMENT
RAYMOND CARVER

And did you get what
you wanted from this life, even so?
I did.
And what did you want?
To call myself beloved, to feel myself
beloved on the earth.

ROSES
VIVIANA FIORENTINO

In my mind
I can still tend the rose garden
of my childhood –
inside me, as if it is my blood
as if it is serum, pulsing, season
on season.

Back then, at the shore
beach-tar on my feet,
I was a child,
but a space remained,
plump, pink, liminal and pure
between its cloying stain
and the life in me.

Life happens this way –
that even now
when I am at risk of drowning
I close my lips tight
against the pressing saltwater
my head tilting backwards
refusing to breathe in
and I am surfacing, like the call

of oystercatchers
piping after the rain,
a pool of pure joy, or like
Socrates'
swans, full throated and defiant
singing,
I have lived.
I have lived.

XXVII. TO-DO LIST
JOHN O'LEARY

To-Do List:
1. find dragon and slay
2. exorcise cat
3. prove conclusively the identity

    of Beauty and Truth.
4. watch, fast and pray
5. sail Atlantic single-handed
6. write name in water

7. return Teach Yourself Waltzing Tape
8. weep for Adonais and feel bad
9. write her a letter telling her
    you love her

10. go out into the midnight
    and check new stars.

AGAINST THE CLOCK
DEREK MAHON

Writing against the clock, the flying calendar,
not to a regular but to a final deadline
(life is short and time, the great reminder,
closes the file of new poems in line
for the printer and binder),

you think of those who wrestled with language
until dementia or whatever struck –
old lads, old girls, the poets of old age
who scribbled on at the unfinished work
with undiminished courage.

Don't give up or give in. Sophocles, obviously,
who wrote Colonnus in his ninetieth year
is our exemplar; and persistent Ovid,
relegated for life to a distant shore,
who fought on for a reprieve.

So many exiles! So many reprobates! –
for whom, to their credit, it was never over:
Dante and Coleridge, Hugo, Whitman, Yeats,
and persecuted, proud Akhmatova
who sang to the black nights.

There are those grim moments when you think
contemporary paper games too daft for you,
not serious, and real values on the blink –
a naff culture not worth contributing to,
time to go back on the drink,

and the old faces turn to you in disgust:
'You're here for the one purpose and one only,
to give us of your best even if your best
is rubbish and your personal testimony
of little general interest.

'You thought you'd done, the uneven output
finished at last, but that wasn't the end,
 was it, since we're obliged to stick it out
until the poem falls from the trembling hand;
so just get on with it.'

As SAFÓ
CAITRÍONA NÍ CHLEIRCHÍN

Deir daoine áirithe gurb é an radharc is áille ar domhan
ná airm ar mhuin capaill, airm ar a cosa nó cabhlach
    loinge
ach deirim gurb é an rud is ansa leat.

From SAPPHO
CAITRÍONA NÍ CHLEIRCHÍN

Some say that the most beautiful sight in the world
is a fleet of ships, an army or horsemen
but I say it is what the heart desires.

HAIKU
GABRIEL ROSENSTOCK

grian an tráthnóna
á lorg féin
i measc linnet

evening sun ...
looking for itself
among *pools*

...

tost ...
díreach sula nglaoitear
chun urnaí sinn

silence ...
just before
the call to prayer

THE DARKLING THRUSH
THOMAS HARDY

I leant upon a coppice gate
When Frost was spectre-grey,
And Winter's dregs made desolate
    The weakening eye of day.
The tangled bine-stems scored the sky
    Like strings of broken lyres,
And all mankind that haunted nigh
    Had sought their household fires.

The land's sharp features seemed to be
    The Century's corpse outleant,
His crypt the cloudy canopy,
    The wind his death-lament.
The ancient pulse of germ and birth
    Was shrunken hard and dry,
And every spirit upon earth
    Seemed fervourless as I.

At once a voice arose among
    The bleak twigs overhead
In a full-hearted evensong
    Of joy illimited;
An aged thrush, frail, gaunt and small,
    In blast-beruffled plume,

Had chosen thus to fling his soul
    Upon the growing gloom.

So little cause for carolings
    Of such ecstatic sound
Was written on terrestrial things
    Afar or nigh around,
That I could think there trembled through
    His happy good-night air
Some blessed Hope, whereof he knew
    And I was unaware.

'HOPE' IS THE THING WITH FEATHERS
EMILY DICKINSON

'Hope' is the thing with feathers –
That perches in the soul –
And sings the tune without the words –
And never stops – at all –

And sweetest – in the Gale – is heard –
And sore must be the storm –
That could abash the little Bird
That kept so many warm –

I've heard it in the chillest land –
And on the strangest Sea –
Yet – never – in Extremity,
It asked a crumb – of me.

CONTINUITIES
WALT WHITMAN

Nothing is ever really lost, or can be lost,
No birth, identity, form – no object of the world.
Nor life, nor force, nor any visible thing;
Appearances must not foil, not shifted sphere confuse
    thy brain.
Ample are time and space—ample the fields of Nature.
The body, sluggish, aged, cold—the embers left from
    earlier fires,
The light in the eye grown dim, shall duly flame again;
The sun now low in the west rises for mornings and for
    noons continual;
To frozen clods ever the spring's invisible law returns,
With grass and flowers and summer fruits and corn.

WHAT THE HANDS KNOW
SUPRIYA KAUR DHALIWAL

Apostrophes crocheted together
nebulously, in a line of music.

There is music in an origami hand—
the tempo of each fold, dictated

by the force of our fingers. The potter's
fingers know how not to press too hard.

The gardener's fingers, however, know
how hard to press / as if this pressing

is a lesson in the management
of sorrows. The hands' approach

to life is more visceral than anything
else. Look at the hands of a lover,

a surgeon, a seamstress, a mother,
a mason, a mathematician, an infant

or Vincent van Gogh. These hands know
how to be generous without spilling

what should not be spilt. Look
how the poets taught us not to misplace

even an apostrophe, fearing
to disturb the music

of the most overused word.

*

When a cloud overshadows a full moon,
we tend to believe it must be a crescent.

*

When a hand holds another hand—
this curation of touch, we know,

is most integral to the existence
of the plural form of hand.

TO MY DEAR AND LOVING HUSBAND
ANNE BRADSTREET

If ever two were one, then surely we;
If ever man were loved by wife, then thee;
If ever wife was happy in a man,
Compare with me, ye women, if you can.
I prize thy love more than whole mines of gold,
Or all the riches that the East doth hold.
My love is such that rivers cannot quench.
Nor aught but love from thee give recompense.
Thy love is such I can no way repay;
The heavens reward thee manifold, I pray.
Then while we live, in love let's so persevere
That when we live no more we may live ever.

SIOLLABADH
SEÁN Ó RÍORDÁIN

Bhí banaltra in otharlann
    I ngile an tráthnóna,
Is cuisleanna i leapachaibh
    Ag preabarnaigh go tomhaiste,
Do sheas sí os gach leaba
    Agus d'fhan sí seal ag comhaireamh
Is do bhreac sí síos an mheadaracht
    Bhí ag siollabadh ina meoraibh,
Is do shiollaib sí go rithimeach
    Fé dheireadh as an seomra,
Is d'fhág 'na diaidh mar chlaisceadal
    Na cuisleanna ag comhaireamh:
Ansin do leath an tAngelus
    Im-shiollabchrith ar bheolaibh,
Ach do tháinig éag ar Amenibh
    Mar chogarnach sa tseomra:
Do leanadh leis an gcantaireacht
    I mainistir na feola,
Na cuisleanna mar mhanachaibh
    Ag siollabadh na nónta.

SYLLABLING

SEÁN Ó RÍORDÁIN

Translated by David Wheatley

A nurse on her round
    One bright afternoon,
Her patients' pulses
    Throbbing like metronomes;
She stood a while counting
    Over each bed, noting down
The metre that syllabled
    Between her fingers
Before syllabling out
    The door, most rhythmically,
Leaving a chorus of
    Pulses counting behind;
Then the Angelus
    Sounded, syllable–
Shaking each lip,
    Amens fading to a whisper
Round the room; and
    On the chanting went
In the monastery of flesh,
    The pulses like monks
Syllabling their nones.

'Ní chodlaím istoíche' –
Beag an rá, ach an bhfionnfar choíche
Ar shúile oscailte
Ualach na hoíche?

From MARY HOGAN'S QUATRAINS

MÁIRE MHAC AN TSAOI

Translated by James Gleasure

'I do not sleep at night' –
Of no account, but will we ever know
With open eyes
The burden of the night?

From REQUIEM: PROLOGUE

ANNA AKHMATOVA

Translated by Seán Dunne

It certainly isn't me.
It must be someone else for I
could never bear such suffering.
Take this thing and bury it.
Take away the lamps
and leave the night.

FEAR

CIARAN CARSON

I fear the vast dimensions of eternity.
I fear the gap between the platform and the train.
I fear the onset of a murderous campaign.
I fear the palpitations caused by too much tea.

I fear the drawn pistol of a rapparee.
I fear the books will not survive the acid rain.
I fear the ruler and the blackboard and the cane.
I fear the Jabberwock, whatever it might be.

I fear the bad decisions of a referee.
I fear the only recourse is to plead insane.
I fear the implications of a lawyer's fee.

I fear the gremlins that have colonized my brain.
I fear to read the small print of the guarantee.
And what else do I fear? Let me begin again.

As FEIS

NUALA NÍ DHOMHNAILL

Nuair a dh'fágas tú
ag an gcé anocht
d'oscail trinse ábhalmhór
istigh im ucht
chomh doimhin sin
ná líonfar
fiú dá ndáilfí
as aon tsoitheach
Sruth na Maoile, Muir Éireann
agus Muir nIocht.

From CARNIVAL
NUALA NÍ DHOMHNAILL

Translated by Paul Muldoon

When I left you
at the quay tonight
an enormous trench opened up
in my core
so profound
it would not be filled
even if you were to pour
from one utensil
the streams of the Mull of Kintyre
and the Irish Sea and the English Channel.

MATAMAITIC DO SHIANSA ÁR N-ANAMA
CEAITÍ NÍ BHEILDIÚIN

CAOINEADH

deor
deor
deor
deora

CAOINEADH AG DUL I LÉIG

ar deoraíocht
deoraí
deora
deor
deo
de'

SEANRITHIM

bualadh
bualadh
bualadh shoc na hinneonach

bualadh
bualadh
bualadh shoc na hinneonach

CUISLE NA MAIDINE

braon
braon drúchta
braon drúchta

braon
braon drúchta
braon draíochta

FORAS

cloch
ar dhá chloch
dhá chloch
ar chloch

MATHEMATICS TO SOUND OUR SOULS
CEAITÍ NÍ BHEILDIÚIN

A CRY

tear
tear
tear
tears

A DIMINISHING CRY

tears of an outcast
tearaway
tearful
tears
tear
tea
    no end

ARCHAIC RHYTHM

beating
beating
beating on the anvil

beating
beating
beating on the anvil

PULSE OF MORNING

drop
drop of dew
drop of dew

drop
drop of dew
drop of magic

STEADY

one stone
on two stones
two stones
on one

ECH DAY ME COMËTH TYDINGES THRE
ANONYMOUS (MEDIEVAL)

Ech day me comëth tydinges thre,
For wel swithë sore ben he:
The on is that Ich shal hennë,
That other that Ich not whennë,
The thriddë is my mestë carë,
That Ich not whider Ich shal fare.

EACH DAY BRINGS THE SAME THREE TALKING POINTS

ANONYMOUS (MEDIEVAL)

Translated by Paul Muldoon

Each day brings the same three talking points
that leave me exceedingly out of joint;
the first is knowing I'll soon depart,
the second not knowing when I'll start,
the third (the cause of my greatest heartache),
not knowing which route I'll take.

AFTER SEPTEMBER
NICOLA GEDDES

These are the lonely days of the far shore
A restless ocean staggers and churns
between me and all my grieving kin
Cries lost in the ruthless gale
These are the salt-sting days of remembering

Shelter me on the island
Gather me in soft lilac wool
Fill my hands with painted eggs
Remind me of the tender days
before loss crashed through the glass
and flooded all our stories.

IMMORTALITY

GEORGE RUSSELL (AE)

We must pass like smoke or live within the spirit's fire;
For we can no more than smoke unto the flame return
If our thought has changed to dream, our will unto
    desire,
    As smoke we vanish though the fire may burn.

Lights of infinite pity star the grey dusk of our days:
Surely here is soul: with it we have eternal breath:
In the fire of love we live, or pass by many ways,
    By unnumbered ways of dream to death.

From NIL NIL
DON PATERSON

In short, this is where you get off, reader;
I'll continue alone, on foot, in the failing light,
following the trail as it steadily fades
into road-repairs, birdsong, the weather, nirvana,
the plot thinning down to a point so refined
not even the angels could dance on it. Goodbye.

HAIKU
GABRIEL ROSENSTOCK

croí éadrom
ag eitilt tríd an saol seo ...
féileacán bánghorm

a light heart
floating through this world ...
a pale blue butterfly

blessing the boats
LUCILLE CLIFTON

(at St. Mary's)

may the tide
that is entering even now
the lip of our understanding
carry you out
beyond the face of fear
may you kiss
the wind then turn from it
certain that it will
love your back   may you
open your eyes to water
water waving forever
and may you in your innocence
sail through this to that

TAKE CARE
MICHAEL D. HIGGINS

In the journey to the light,
the dark moments
should not threaten.
Belief
requires
that you hold steady.
Bend, if you will,
with the wind.
The tree is your teacher,
roots at once
more firm
from experience
in the soil
made fragile.

Your gentle dew will come
and a stirring
of power
to go on
towards the space
of sharing.

In the misery of the I,
in rage,

it is easy to cry out
against all others
but to weaken
is to die
in the misery of knowing
the journey abandoned
towards the sharing
of all human hope
and cries
is the loss
of all we know
of the divine
reclaimed
for our shared
humanity.
Hold firm.
Take care.
Come home
together.

WINTER SOLSTICE PASSAGE GRAVE AT NEWGRANGE

CATHERINE ANN CULLEN

The chamber's heart is thrown a line of light
Once in the year. Out of the darkest days,
Astronomy, arithmetic effect this bright
Miracle, turning cold light to blaze,
Grey tomb to womb where a new year is kindled.
Heart, drink your fill of light: the darkness dwindles.

YOUR NATIVE HOME
GIULIANO NISTRI

You asked me once,
'Where does the wind go?'
I will tell you now.

After it gathers the murmuring sails
Of all the boats in the sea and tugs them to harbour
And lifts every coloured kite in the field,

After it herds the wayward clouds
Back into the sky-pen and spreads the softened pollen
Over the crust of this earth,

After it delivers each longing seed
To its solitary furrow and whistles down
The flute of resting chimneys,

After it mills the wheat in the long-shadowed farmlands
And stretches out to clink the chimes
That hang by a thread on summer porches,

After it swivels the iron-cast weathervanes to caw
Like roosters and sweeps the camphorous leaves
Into the wet ditch,

After it combs the morning fields
And braids the crowns
Of darkening forests,

After it dries yesterday's clothes on your line
And nuzzles around the working nose
Of your sleeping dog,

It finally goes home, where you came from,
And carries your father and mother
To their long-awaited sleep.

OUR REVELS NOW ARE ENDED
WILLIAM SHAKESPEARE

Our revels now are ended. These our actors,
As I foretold you were all spirits and
Are melted into air, into thin air:
And, like the baseless fabric of this vision,
The cloud-capped towers, the gorgeous palaces,
The solemn temples, the great globe itself,
Yea, all of which it inherit, shall dissolve,
And, like this insubstantial pageant faded,
Leave not a rack behind. We are such stuff
As dreams are made on, and our little life
Is rounded with a sleep.

SNOWDROPS

LOUISE GLÜCK

Do you know what I was, how I lived? You know
what despair is; then
winter should have meaning for you.

I did not expect to survive,
earth suppressing me. I didn't expect
to waken again, to feel
in damp earth my body
able to respond again, remembering
after so long how to open again
in the cold light
of earliest spring –

afraid, yes, but among you again
crying yes risk joy

in the raw wind of the new world.

FÁS AGUS BÁS

DANNY SHEEHY

Chuireas ar mo shuaimhneas inniu
ag éisteacht le méileach na gcaorach.
le cantaireacht ghlórmhar na n-éan
is le hanáil fáiscithe na farraige
deich gcrann is trí fichid,
naoi gcrann is daichead fearnóige.
crann do gach lá na seachtaine
ar feadh deich seachtaine.

Bhraitheas taise an fháís,
chonac úire na hithreach
d'fháisceas an chré im' dhorn.
Fuaireas fuinneamh as an saothrú
síothlóga a chur mar bhuíochas
go raibh beatha sa talamh
mar go rabhas ag sá síos
chun an fás a fháscadh aníos
mar is aisti aníos a thagann
gach fás ag slánú ár mbeatha.

Shamhlaíos nuair a bheidh
na crainn fásta fé dhuilliúir ghlasa
go mbeadsa críonna ach fós im' bheathaidh

ach nuair a chuirfear mo chorp sa chill
is nuair a dhéanfaidh cré do mo chnámha
an gcuimhneoidh éinne gur
chuireas crann ag fás
nú gur chuireas dán ar phár
ar son an bháis.

GROWING AND DYING

DANNY SHEEHY

Translated by Alan Titley

While I listened today
To the bleating of the sheep
And the glorious singing of the birds
And the tightening breath of the sea
I planted at my leisure
A full seventy trees in all,
Forty-nine of them alders,
One tree for every day of the week
Through ten long weeks.

I felt the sap of growth
Saw the freshness of the earth
Squeezed the clay in my fist.
Soaking up energy from the labour
Of putting seedlings down
To give thanks for the life in the ground
As I thrust deep to bring growth
Up from below, as it is from there
That growth springs to save our lives.

I began to think that when the trees
Came forth in their fresh green leaves

That I would be old, but still alive,
But when my body was laid to rest
And my bones had turned to dust
Would anybody remember
That I had planted trees to grow
Or that I had written a poem
For the sake of death.

THE PARTING GLASS
TRADITIONAL

Of all the money that e'er I had,
I spent it in good company;
And all the harm I've ever done,
Alas it was to none but me.
And all I've done for want of wit,
To memory now I can't recall.
So fill to me the parting glass
Good night and joy be to you all

So fill to me the parting glass
And drink a health whate'er befall,
And gently rise and softly call
Good night and joy be to you all.

TO EVERY THING THERE IS A SEASON
ECCLESIASTES 3 1-8

1. To everything there is a season, and a time to every purpose under the heaven:
2. A time to be born, and a time to die; a time to plant, and a time to pluck up that which is planted;
3. A time to kill, and a time to heal; a time to break down, and a time to build up;
4. A time to weep, and a time to laugh; a time to mourn, and a time to dance;
5. A time to cast away stones, and a time to gather stones together; a time to embrace, and a time to refrain from embracing;
6. A time to get, and a time to lose; a time to keep, and a time to cast away;
7. A time to rend, and a time to sew; a time to keep silence, and a time to speak;
8. A time to love, and a time to hate; a time of war, and a time of peace.

PART 2:
POEMS FOR CARERS AND THE BEREAVED

THE SICK BIRD
JOHN MONTAGUE

I

Cycling along the Clogher road
Master MacGurren found a sick bird.
He brought it to me, sick in bed,
and it lay, in a rag-lined shoe box,
within reach of my caressing hand.

After a few days, it learnt to respond
to the touch of a warm finger
on its fragile head, bruised feathers.
Its claws were crisp as winter twigs
and its small heart hammered:
minute, intense, terrible.

One morning I was better, and
so was my little companion, hungry
beak gaping on the pillow beside me.
I cupped it in my palms and,
cradling it to the window, hoisted
and helped it fly away.

II
Thirty years later, I find a bird
on the road's edge, outside Ballydehob:
a coal tit, meantán dubh.
I place its delicate body inside
my shirt, as I cycle home,
to show it to my children.

Now it rests on the unlit stove
in a cushioned box, beside where I write,
inspected, every so often, by tiptoeing children.
Its heart still furiously beating;
when will it take flight?

RED BROCADE
NAOMI SHIHAB NYE

The Arabs used to say,
When a stranger appears at your door,
feed him for three days
before asking who he is,
where he's come from,
where he's headed.
That way, he'll have strength
enough to answer.
Or, by then you'll be
such good friends
you don't care.

Let's go back to that.
Rice? Pine nuts?
Here, take the red brocade pillow.
My child will serve water
to your horse.

No, I was not busy when you came!
I was not preparing to be busy.
That's the armor everyone put on
to pretend they had a purpose
in the world.

I refuse to be claimed.
Your plate is waiting.
We will snip fresh mint
into your tea.

MIRACLE
SEAMUS HEANEY

Not the one who takes up his bed and walks
But the ones who have known him all along
And carry him in —

Their shoulders numb, the ache and stoop deeplocked
In their backs, the stretcher handles
Slippery with sweat. And no let up

Until he's strapped on tight, made tiltable
and raised to the tiled roof, then lowered for healing.
Be mindful of them as they stand and wait

For the burn of the paid-out ropes to cool,
Their slight lightheadedness and incredulity
To pass, those ones who had known him all along.

LAMENT
MOYA CANNON

Let me learn from the Brent geese
their grey grammar of grief
as they wheel in a bow-backed flock
onto a February tide.

Let me learn from these strong geese
to map my losses with a cry,
learn from those who are always losing
a chick, a lover or a brother,
losing one cold country or another.

Let me learn from the black-necked geese
how to bend my shoulders low
over a wrack-draped shore,
let me learn from the curlew's long weep,
Oh, oh, oh, oh, oh.

A BLACKTHORN WINTER

ANN LEAHY

The funeral done, we walked in bright, expectant April
on lanes that wound to the crumbling burial ground.
Ash trees, hung with last year's wretched seeds in tatters,
waved like beggars eager to converse. All we heard
was a rattle as the wind exhaled through each.

Too weak to stand, she'd seemed not desolate but
    amazed:
'imagine me, *me* who could fork reeks of hay drawn in
by men, *me* who could do the work of any of them?'
As if this day – her last – was the first on which she'd
    noticed
any change: decades had shrunk to a season.

Spring was stark. Blackthorn in arthritic tangles
occupied a nether region, leafless, yet pricked
with hard-nosed buds in pink, caught between
death and regeneration, as if the year
was loath to burgeon again within the bark.

By Month's Mind, roads were fringed with Queen Anne's
    lace
in frothy umbels thrust on thin, frail arms

to buffet every car that passed in futile gestures
of embrace. Petals clung for weeks like wings
ripped from death's spectral insects. Who could forget?

We'd stood then, sure of death, not sure when, while
    buds
on midnight's trees were seared with frost. And
    mutterings of love
perished, half-formed, as we composed ourselves by
    the bed.
At last, a gasp, then a pause. But who knows what shrill,
silent screech? What soft, billowing updraft? In the end,
    no words.

The graveyard's unkempt edge was faintly sibilant
by summer's close with blades of Yorkshire Fog
that bowed before the wind's blunt scythe.
Then that dissolute breeze withdrew to leave
them leaning, not quite touching, hushed and askew.

From CHURCHYARD VIEW: THE NEW ESTATE

DENNIS O'DRISCOLL

the blackness of
the cemetery blackbird,
its song an octave lower

DO NOT ASK: IN MEMORY OF PHILIP CASEY, 4-2-2018

NESSA O'MAHONY

We didn't plan for it,
but these past days
we've stalked death,
as we wandered streets,
looked up at domes,
tried to remember the past
without googling it.

Skulls everywhere:
on market stalls,
behind glass in the ritz
of Burlington arcade,
bells tolling the footfall.

Then the pink room,
where Keats spotted red,
signed his death warrant
in a four-poster bed.

And here, now, returned
to our borrowed bed
in the shades of St Paul's,

we take our beat
from the chimes,
till the phone beeps
with the news.

You'd have seen the joke;
were always the first
to try out new technology,
to match it to old words.

Another bell:
and I know
for whom it tolled,
old friend.

LIVES

GERARD SMYTH

In memory of Ethel Smith

That morning it was news of your death that woke me.
The night before I had noticed that my bedside book
was almost at the end of the story.
Even in dull January you could see the bright side,
wherever it was – behind the rain
or in dismal shade, when the day was one of
    disappointment.

In a room half-lit by candle-flicker you died before the
    death
of winter. And when you died we lifted you up,
six shoulders carrying a tireless dancer.
Nothing remains undone – one life was all you needed.
And what would you want from us?
Nothing except that we who live on
should hum the happier tune and not the lament or
    fugue.

From THE ARCHITECT
JAKI MCCARRICK

'I have a journey, sir, shortly to go;
my master calls me, I must not say no.'
— *Kent, King Lear, v., iii*

i.m. Michael Mehremitch

Three months after your scattering,
on New Year's Day,
I walk along Templetown and Shelling Hill.

The light is warm and white
and a happy three-legged dog
wanders the beach, ownerless.

The water is slow and winter-blue
and I sense you out there,
as far as a sea-mile, and closer,

lingering on the water's edge,
in the trapped plumes
of foam in rockpools.

And you are present, too,
in the spirituous air,
not yet gone from where you'd been scattered.

By the beach-end I pick up two mussel shells
and declare them last-trace mementoes,
like old postcards, or poems.

As ATHAIR AGUS INÍON

AIFRIC MAC AODHA

Réalt

D'Inis sé di gur thit
Réalt ón spéir anuas
Isteach sa phróca
A chóirigh sé
Ar thairseach
A fuinneoige.

Go fóill féin
Ni bhainfeadh sí
An barr de
Ar fhaitíos
Go n-éalódh
Orthu.

Olann

Mar bhlúirín uainolla
É i bhfostú i ndriseog:
Siúd mar a mhairfeadh
A ghrá di.

From FATHER AND DAUGHTER
AIFRIC MAC AODHA

Star
He told her
a star fell
from the sky
into the jar
he had placed
on the window-sill.

Even now,
she would not remove
the lid
for fear
it should escape on them.

Wool
Like a scrap of a lamb's wool
entangled in a briar:
so would survive
his love for her.

A MAN FROM DERRYBRIEN
PATRICK DEELEY

He had the shoulders of a horse, and the long face
of a horse, and the belly of a horse.
He clomped in his wet-concrete boots as might a horse.
He whinnied for a laugh. Threw the head
at this notion or that, flighty, suspicious as a horse.
Hired himself out in the name of a horse.
And shouted, if you were a mate of his, 'Hello, horse.'
Hauled a horse-load hour after hour,
and drank by night as became a thirsty horse.
Put his money on a losing horse. Shod
and groomed himself to make 'the odd gallop back
     across'.
Otherwise 'lived horse and got grass', cantering
memories of hills he'd never settle. Lost,
it took forty years, his wind and limb – a broken horse.
In Camden Town. Forgotten as a matter of course.

HOME OF WORSHIP
ABBY OLIVEIRA

You will not enter this home in black.
Leave yon scythe at the door. No need
to paint your face clown-white, your eyes
like void wells. These walls exist

because Life lives here, Life loves here
you, Death, are a guest.

Don't come empty handed; bring whisky & backy
orchids & gerbera daisies, bring a fiddle
play it like the Divil: in this house
we dance.

Speak! None of your silent, dour skulking.
Your stories make everything sacred:

the pen next to the mouldy mug
the CD tray still open
the list on the fridge: bread   butter   milk
        prescriptions.

Remove your battered boots, wash your feet:
you are entering a home of worship.

AND SOUL
EAVAN BOLAND

My mother died one summer—
the wettest in the records of the state.
Crops rotted in the west.
Checked tablecloths dissolved in back gardens.
Empty deck chairs collected rain.
As I took my way to her
through traffic, through lilacs dripping blackly
behind houses
and on curbsides, to pay her
the last tribute of a daughter, I thought of something
I remembered
I heard once, that the body is, or is
said to be, almost all
water and as I turned southward, that ours is
a city of it,
one in which
every single day the elements begin
a journey towards each other that will never,
given our weather,
fail—
     the ocean visible in the edges cut by it,
cloud colour reaching into air,
the Liffey storing one and summoning the other,

salt greeting the lack of it at the North Wall and,
as if that wasn't enough, all of it
ending up almost every evening
inside our speech—
coast canal ocean river stream and now
mother and I drove on and although
the mind is unreliable in grief, at
the next cloudburst it almost seemed
they could be shades of each other,
the way the body is
of every one of them and now
they were on the move again—fog into mist,
mist into sea spray and both into the oily glaze
that lay on the railings of
the house she was dying in
as I went inside.

MEMORY OF MY FATHER
PATRICK KAVANAGH

Every old man I see
Reminds me of my father
When he had fallen in love with death
One time when sheaves were gathered.

That man I saw in Gardiner Street
Stumble on the kerb was one,
He stared at me half-eyed,
I might have been his son.

And I remember the musician
Faltering over his fiddle
In Bayswater, London,
He too set me the riddle.

Every old man I see
In October-coloured weather
Seems to say to me:
'I was once your father.'

NIGHT DRIVE
TOM FRENCH

The closest, Mother, we have been in years
was a night drive back from Achill on our own.
Our tyres pressed the smooth cheeks to the ice,
gripping nothing, squealing, barely holding on.

Something stepped into our beam and stood there,
dumbly, ready to confront its death.
I remember your right hand in the darkness –
a white bird frightened from its fastness

in your lap, bracing yourself for the impact,
hearing you whisper *Jesus* under your breath,
preparing your soul for the moment of death.
Then, just as suddenly, nothing happened –

the sheep stepped back into the verge
for no reason, attracted by a clump of grass.
For days I felt the pressure of your hand on mine.
You would've led me to the next world, Mother, like a
    child.

FATHER AND SON
F.R. HIGGINS

Only last week, walking the hushed fields
Of our most lovely Meath, now thinned by November,
I came to where the road from Laracor leads
To the Boyne river–that seems more lake than river,
Stretched in uneasy light and stript of reeds.

And walking longside an old weir
Of my people's, where nothing stirs–only the shadowed
Leaden flight of a heron up the lean air–
I went unmanly with grief, knowing how my father,
Happy though captive in years, walked last with me
     there.

Yes, happy in Meath with me for a day
He walked, taking stock of herds hid in their own
     breathing;
And naming colts, gusty as wind, once steered by his
     hand,
Lightnings winked in the eyes that were half shy in
     greeting
Old friends–the wild blades, when he gallivanted the
     land.

For that proud, wayward man now my heart breaks–
Breaks for that man whose mind was a secret eyrie,
Whose kind hand was sole signet of his race,
Who curbed me, scorned my green ways, yet
    increasingly loved me
Till Death drew its grey blind down his face.

And yet I am pleased that even my reckless ways
Are living shades of his rich calms and passions–
Witnesses for him and for those faint namesakes
With whom now he is one, under yew branches,
Yes, one in a graven silence no bird breaks.

MA
PAUL MULDOON

Old photographs would have her bookish, sitting
Under a willow. I take that to be croquet
Lawn. She reads aloud, no doubt from Rupert Brooke.
The month is always May or June.

Or with the stranger on the motor-bike.
Not my father, no. This one's all crew-cut
And polished brass buttons.
An American soldier, perhaps.
                    And the full moon
Swaying over Keenaghan, the orchards and the cannery,
Thins to a last yellow-hammer, and goes.
The neighbours gather, all Keenaghan and Collegelands.
There is story-telling. Old miners in Coalisland
Going into the ground. Swinging, for fear of the gas,
The soft flame of a canary.

IN MEMORY OF MY MOTHER

PATRICK KAVANAGH

I do not think of you lying in the wet clay
Of a Monaghan graveyard; I see
You walking down a lane among the poplars
On your way to the station, or happily

Going to second Mass on a summer Sunday –
You meet me and you say:
'Don't forget to see about the cattle –'
Among your earthiest words the angels stray.

And I think of you walking along a headland
Of green oats in June,
So full of repose, so rich with life –
And I see us meeting at the end of a town

On a fair day by accident, after
The bargains are all made and we can walk
Together through the shops and stalls and markets
Free in the oriental streets of thought.

O you are not lying in the wet clay,
For it is a harvest evening now and we
Are piling up the ricks against the moonlight
And you smile up at us – eternally.

THE LUCK

PAULA MEEHAN

I don't do the past, said my father,
into my oldfashioned microphone.
The rain, the eternal Irish rain,
beats and beats and beats at the window
and the fattening geese are dreaming
of the north. I knew that he'd be dead
by Samhain when the geese returned again.
We bet online and watched the horses,
all going round the bend together.

CAFÉ
THEO DORGAN

In the entire boom and confusion
of the café, one point of stillness:
a man reading over and over
the last letter received from his dead father.

As MARBHNADH CHEARBHALLÁIN AR BHÁS A MHNÁ, MÁIRE NIC UIDHIR

TOIRDHEALBHACH Ó CEARBHALLÁIN

Leagan le hAifric Mac Aodha

Intleacht na hÉireann, na Gréige 's na Róimhe,
Bíodh uile in éineacht in aon bheairtín romhamsa:
Ghlacfainn mar fhéirín thar an méid sin de na seoda,
Máire ón Éirne a's mé féin a bheith dá pógadh.

Is tuirseach tinn tréithlag mé féin gach tráthnóna,
'S ar maidin ag éirí mar a d'éag uaim mo nuachar;
Dá bhfaighinn anois tréada 's gach saibhreas dár nósadh,
Ní ghlacfainn ina dhiaidh sin aon bhean le pósadh.

Fuair mé seal in Éirinn go haerach 's go sóúil,
Ag ól le gach tréanfhear a bhí éifeachtach ceolmhar,
Fágadh ina dhiaidh sin liom féin mé go brónach,
I ndeireadh mo shaoil 's gan mo chéile a bheith beo
    agam.

From O'CAROLAN'S LAMENT FOR HIS WIFE, MARY MAGUIRE

TOIRDHEALBHACH Ó CEARBHALLÁIN

Interpreted by Aifric Mac Aodha

I'd give up all the world's learning to simply hold her.
The sun goes down and dawn brings sorrow.
My love is gone. What else was there?

DAIDIA
CAITLÍN NIC ÍOMHAIR

Is creidim fós go bhféadfainn é a mhealladh ar ais
     chugam
ar shiúl róghar don uisce dom,
is gurb é atá do mo thionlacan síos pasáiste dorcha
     istoíche,
scian chosanta lena ucht.
Agus uaireanta, fiú, thabharfainn mion an leabhair,
agus a bhfuil ann de dhíomá orm faoi,
go ligeann sé osna taobh liom istoíche
ag tál trua nuair a thitim,
ag gairdeas as mo ghaisce
is ag caoineadh mo ghlaise.

Agus creidim fós,
i ndáiríre píre,
thíos faoin amhras is faoin uabhar
i gcroílár mo phutóige,
creidim,
i ngach macmhóid nach ann dó,
nach faide uaim é ná sa ghluaisteán a théann tharam
nó an cruth faoi charn nótaí le m'ais sa leabharlann
an fear seo a chum mé
is a cheap mé
is a chaill mé.

DADDY

CAITLÍN NIC ÍOMHAIR

Translated by Colette Bryce

I still believe I could lure him back
if I edge too close to the water,
that it's him by my side in the dark alley,
blade at his chest, ready to defend me.
And sometimes
I'd even swear on the bible,
for all its disappointments,
that he sighs by my bed in the night,
the first to commiserate
when I trip up,
to applaud my successes,
mourning my innocence.

Yes, I believe,
deep down in my gut
beneath all pride and rational doubt,
and each polite avowal that he's gone,
that he's not much further away from me
than a passing car
or the shadow thrown
by this pile of drafts accruing
in the library,

this man who made me,
who dreamt me up
and who lost me.

From A PART OF OURSELVES

PETER FALLON

He'll die again at Christmas every year.
We felt the need grow all night
to give him a name, to assert him
as a member of our care, to say he was
alive. Oh, he lived all right,

he lived a lifetime. Now certain sounds,
sights and smells are the shibboleth
of a season. In the hospital corridor
I held him in my arms. I held him tight.
His mother and I, we held our breath –

and he held his.

From CLEARANCES

SEAMUS HEANEY

i.m. M.K.H., 1911–1984

2

Polished linoleum shone there. Brass taps shone.
The china cups were very white and big—
An unchipped set with sugar bowl and jug.
The kettle whistled. Sandwich and tea scone
Were present and correct. In case it run,
The butter must be kept out of the sun.
And don't be dropping crumbs. Don't tilt your chair.
Don't reach. Don't point. Don't make noise when you stir.

It is Number 5, New Row, Land of the Dead,
Where grandfather is rising from his place
With spectacles pushed back on a clean bald head
To welcome a bewildered homing daughter
Before she even knocks. 'What's this? What's this?'
And they sit down in the shining room together.

3

When all the others were away at Mass
I was all hers as we peeled potatoes.
They broke the silence, let fall one by one
Like solder weeping off the soldering iron:
Cold comforts set between us, things to share
Gleaming in a bucket of clean water.
And again let fall. Little pleasant splashes
From each other's work would bring us to our senses.
So while the parish priest at her bedside
Went hammer and tongs at the prayers for the dying
And some were responding and some crying
I remembered her head bent towards my head,
Her breath in mine, our fluent dipping knives–
Never closer the whole rest of our lives.

DÁN DOM ATHAIR
MICHAEL KIRBY

Gluais ort, a Dhaid,
Ardóimid ár seolta sí
Go bhfágfam an cuan seo.
Leagse a thosach le gaoth.
Ciorraigh an siota
Go luífidh a sliasta anonn
Ag tabhairt guala
Do shúistí bog cúrach
Thar ríocht na dtonn.

Mise agus tusa, a Dhaid,
Agus Dia inár dteannta,
Réalt eolais an Mhoil
Ag rince ós ár gcrann,
Gach leoithne bog ceolmhar
Ag seinm ar théada teann,
Sinn ag bogadh abhaile
Gan bhárthainn
Thar ríocht na dtonn.

TO MY FATHER
MICHAEL KIRBY

Only us both,
You and I,
With God
Up on high,
The wing
Of the gull,
The cloud,
The star
In the sky.
The soft surging
Seas,
The night
And a new dawn
In store.
The beacons
Are lighting us home
To Heaven's bright shore.

WHY HAVE YE NO ROUTHE ON MY CHILD?

ANONYMOUS (MEDIEVAL)

Why have ye no routhe on my child?
Have routhe on me ful of mourning;
Tak doun o rod my derworth child,
Or prik me o rode with my derling!
More pine ne may me ben y-don
Than lete me live in sorwe and shame;
As love me bindëth to my sone,
So let us deyen bothe y-same.

WHY NOT SHOW SOME PITY FOR MY CHILD?

ANONYMOUS (MEDIEVAL)

Translated by Paul Muldoon

Why not show some pity for my child?
At least show pity for me at my time of loss;
either take down my precious child
or nail me up there with him on the cross. e

Nothing would cause me greater woe
than to live on in sorrow and despair;
since it is love that binds us in our throes
why not let us leave this world as a pair?

MARBHNA OISÍN

PADDY BUSHE

i.m. Oisín O'Mahony, naíonán

Mar gur ar éigin ar shroich tú Tír na nÓg
Sular sciobadh arís siar thar farraige thú
Mar nár thuigis riamh draíocht na dúthaí sin
Ná fós arís a bheith dá ceal
Mar ná rabhais riamh faoi gheasa chinn óir
Ná aon chapall bhán faoi smacht agat
Mar nach raibh agat aon agallamh le seanóirí
Ná seanchas peile, ná camán id lámh agat
Mar gur robáladh an taisce a shamhlaigh d'athair duit
Agus aisling gheal do mháthair
Is id dhiaidhse atáthar, Oisín, is tá an saol ar fad
Titithe as a riocht, mar ghaiscíoch ón diallait.

LAMENT FOR OISÍN

PADDY BUSHE

i.m. Oisín O'Mahony, infant

Because you had barely arrived at Tír na nÓg
Before you were swept back out to sea again;
Because you never realised the magic of that place
Nor yet again what it is to lose it;
Because you were never spellbound by golden hair
Nor held the reins of a white horse in your hands;
Because you had never conversed with old men,
Never talked football, nor gripped a hurley;
Because your father was robbed of the treasure he
        imagined,
And your mother of her brightest dreaming;
We are forlorn, Oisín, and the whole world
Has tumbled to the ground, like a hero from the saddle.

THE LOVER IN WINTER PLAINETH FOR THE SPRING

ANONYMOUS (16TH CENTURY)

O western wind, when wilt thou blow
    That the small rain down can blow?
Christ, that my love were in my arms
    And I in my bed again.

CYBER YOU

JULIE O'CALLAGHAN

I need to see you
living and breathing.
I go to YouTube
and there you are being you
(the tiny you)
with the tie I bought you
for Christmas
sitting on a chair
on a stage in Santa Fe
asking Seamus questions.
Eternally.

As CAOINEADH AIRT UÍ LAOGHAIRE

EIBHLÍN DUBH NÍ CHONAILL (1743–1800)

Mo ghrá thú agus mo rún!
Tá do stácaí ar a mbonn,
Tá do bha buí á gcrú;
is ar mo chroí atá do chumha
ná leigheasfadh Cúige Mumhan
ná Gaibhne Oileáin na bhFionn.
Go dtiocfaidh Art Ó Laoghaire chugham
ní scaipfidh ar mo chumha
atá i lár mo chroí á bhrú,
dúnta suas go dlúth
mar a bheadh glas a bheadh ar thrúnc
's go raghadh an eochair amú.

From THE KEEN FOR ART Ó LAOGHAIRE
EIBHLÍN DUBH NÍ CHONAILL (1743–1800)

Translated by Doireann Ní Ghríofa

O, my love and my darling!
Your barley has risen thick and golden,
your fair cows are well-milked,
but such pain grips my heart still
that all of Munster cannot fix me a remedy,
nor even Fair Island's gifted smithery.
Unless Art Ó Laoghaire returns to me
this grief will never be eased,
it weighs on my heart so brutally,
keeping it sealed so tightly
as a lock clasps a chest
whose golden key has been lost from me.

THE LOSS
JOHN O'DONNELL

You are everywhere I look about this house,
Hiding under chairs or around doorways,
Longed for like a small chance missed

Imagined yet. Giggles from an empty corner;
The bump behind the drapes a wind
Gusting through a broken pane. This is

The still life of your absence, etched
In silence. Ashes in the grate are unsung names
For you; the bowed heads of flowers

Bright bedroom colours I'll unpick
From a vase in the bay window
That today is framing swollen hills and

Clotted darkening streams, the winter
You leave after, a shadow gone through
A gap in the fence only a child could fill.

NOTE
LEANNE O'SULLIVAN

If we become separated from each other
this evening try to remember the last time
you saw me, and go back and wait for me there.
I promise I won't be very long,
though I am haunted by the feeling
that I might keep missing you,
with the noise of the city growing too
loud and the day burning out so quickly.
But let's just say it's as good a plan as any.
Just once let's imagine a word for the memory
that lives beyond the body, that circles
and sets all things alight. For I have
singled you out from the whole world,
and I would – even as the darkness
is falling, even when the night comes
where there are no more words, and the day
comes when there is no more light.

As AN FEAR DÁNA

After M'Anam do Scar Riomsa Aréir
Muiríoch Albanach Ó Dálaigh (c.1220)
ALAN TITLEY

Scaradh anama lem chorp ba ea bás Mhaoil Mheá. An
colann ab ansa liom sa saol san uaigh. Níorbh aonarach
go dtí sin mé, b'olc an saol cam a chonaic mé romham.

Leath mo choirp ann choinneal úr, leath mo shiúil,
leath mo thaobh, leath mo bheatha ar leaba fhuar, leath
mo bháis an banlaoch caomh. Mo chéadghrá a rosc mall
mór, mo dhara grá a malaí donn, déadbhán agus geal a
cliabh, crann taca mo shaoil a chrom.

Leath mo shúl í, leath mo lámh, leath mo bhreithe, leath
mo chroí, leathnaith an mheirtne ar fud mo bhaill, ba í
ceartleath m'anama í.

From AN FEAR DÁNA

On the death of Muiríoch's wife (c. 1220)

ALAN TITLEY

Maol Mheá's death last night ripped my soul from my
body. The body I loved more than any in this world now
in the grave. Never alone was I until now, an aimless life
I see before me.

Half my body that bright candle, half my eyes, half
my side, half my life on a cold slab, half my death that
woman hero. My first love was her deep soft eyes, and
after that her darkling brow, toothwhite clean her gentle
breast, my life support is now gone down.

Half my eyes, half my hands, half my birth,
enfeeblement has gripped my parts, she was fully half
my soul.

THE WIDOW'S LAMENT IN SPRINGTIME
WILLIAM CARLOS WILLIAMS

Sorrow is my own yard
where the new grass
flames as it has flamed
often before but not
with the cold fire
that closes round me this year.
Thirty-five years
I lived with my husband.
The plumtree is white today
with masses of flowers.
Masses of flowers
load the cherry branches
and colour some bushes
yellow and some red
but the grief in my heart
is stronger than they
for though they were my joy
formerly, today I notice them
and turn away forgetting.
Today my son told me
that in the meadows,
at the edge of the heavy woods
in the distance, he saw

trees of white flowers.
I feel that I would like
to go there
and fall into those flowers
and sink into the marsh near them.

POSSIBILITY
DERMOT BOLGER

Just leave yourself open to the possibility
That one dawn you wake to find your mind clear,

One dawn you will win back the love you derailed,
One dawn you will kick the habit of blaming yourself.

One dawn you will wake to hear a clear signal,
A wavelength unmuffled by inference or static,

You will recognize the DJ's voice as your own
Advertising a unique extravaganza treasure hunt
Where each clue is a signpost through your past.

You will walk through a maze of sleeping estates,
Collecting golden tickets concealed amid mistakes
You made when addiction stopped you thinking
        straight.

That dawn, when figures emerge amidst the chaos,
You will walk forward, unafraid to embrace happiness.

BULL ISLAND HAIKU
PAT BORAN

When my best friend died
I came here and sat for hours.
The gulls cried. They cried.

MY SISTER IS NOT A STATISTIC
DOROTHY DUFFY

Tomorrow, when the latest Deathometer of Covid is
    announced in sonorous tones,
While all the bodies still mount and curl towards the
    middle of the curve
Heaped one atop and alongside the other
My sister will be among those numbers, among the
    throwaway lines
Among the platitudes and lowered eyes,
an older person with underlying health conditions,
A pitiful way to lay rest the bare bones of a life.

MY SISTER IS NOT A STATISTIC
Her underlying conditions were
Love
Kindness
Belief in the essential goodness of mankind
Uproarious laughter
Forgiveness
Compassion
A storyteller
A survivor
A comforter
A force of nature
And so much more

MY SISTER IS NOT A STATISTIC

She died without the soft touch of a loved one's hand
Without the feathered kiss upon her forehead
Without the muted murmur of familiar family voices
    gathered around her bed,
Without the gentle roar of laughter that comes with
    memories recalled

Evoked from a time that already seems distant, when
    we were
connected by the simplicity of touch, of voice, of
    presence.

MY SISTER IS NOT A STATISTIC

She was a woman who spanned the seven ages.
A mother
A grandmother
A great grandmother
A sister
A Friend
An aunt
A carer
A giver

MY SISTER IS NOT A STATISTIC

And so, she joins the mounting thousands

THEY ARE NOT STATISTICS ON THE DEATHOMETER OF COVID

They are the wives, mothers, children, fathers, sisters,
brothers

The layers of all our loved ones

If she could, believe me when I say, she would hold every
last one of your loved ones, croon to and comfort
them and say – you were loved.

Whilst we who have been left behind mourn deep,
keening the loss, the injustice, the rage.

One day we will smile and laugh again, we will
remember with joy that, once, we shared a life,
we knew joy and survived sadness.

You are my sister .... and I love you.

MOTHER MOON
ERIKO TSUGAWA-MADDEN

No, you don't blind my eyes like the sun does, so I'll stay
    here
a little longer, until the chill of the night sinks into my
    bones.
Mare Serenitatis, Mare Tranquillitatis, smudged
    topography.
The two mesmeric eyes of a wakeful owl.

Your gaze mellows and glows against the inky blue.
Let me wait until this ripe fruit falls into my cupped
    hands.

I know I'll still find you in the morning, pale in the pale
    sky
softly submerging in the new day nearing.

    That night, in the hospital room, I tried to point out
        to my Mother,
    how enormous and full the moon was.

    I thought she should see it and ... and then ...
        she seemed to have gone.
    I was speaking to her without noticing her going.

A tear, found at the corner of her eye, so small that it
    couldn't
flow and I dried it with my little finger as a nurse
    came rushing in.

Oh, a nurse so kind, who offered to ring my sister for
    me, as I was
just a blank. Now leaving the room so they could
    bathe mother.

One last time I touched her lips, faintly open and
    her teeth
visible, in the crescent gap. Was she about to say that
    she loved me?

Outside, I looked again for the moon. No moon.
Looking in the wrong direction. When I found it, I
    noticed ...

The warden so kind, was watching me out of
concern,
half hiding himself behind the door.

You must have been at perigee that night. So large, you
    startled me.
Your pull pulls oceans and the tide sweeps the beaches
    anew.

Let me walk to the edge of a sickle beach where no
    human trails show
and make my own small leap, like the first man on the
    moon.

Waves coming and going, coming and going. Mother is
    breathing.
Thousands of pebbles all at once roll and whisper in the
    ebbing water.

Plovers synchronised with the wavelets. Another day
    just happens pristine.
How gracefully indifferent the world is about yesterdays.

I am invisible, where among withered brown grasses
on the sand bank, new green grasses mingle and grow.

Wind, waves and sea birds, the polyphony for the
    opening of a day.
Yesterday is absorbed in vast aeons of time.

*

Apogee, they say on another day when your orbit is at its
    farthest.

You deserve that distance from this troubled clamorous
    planet.

On moonless nights, I still imagine your outline above
    me,
until the sun bestows its opulent light upon a new
    moon.

In alignment with the Sun, you're eclipsed by our
    shadow.
A long jetty across space, upon which I walk.

Now moonlight shows up the trickle in the brambled
    ditch and
silvers the dangling tears on the gossamer.

Before coming to my door, you passed many bell towers
    and roofs.
Let me linger a little longer until you slide into those
    amorphous clouds.

*

The Earth is blue ... how wonderful

A young cosmonaut saw our planet floating blue in the
    darkness.
Like him, you see us too. Solitary, in lambent blue.

I trust you moon. Each revolution and return recasts
    our day.
Mare Cognitum, Mare Nectaris ... wise, sweet seas.

No, you have never left me, you haven't. Neither has
    Mother.
We are all bound to the route of your orbit.

SUMMER IN KILLYBEGS
NANDI JOLA

I happened to arrive with the best weather in the wild
    Atlantic way
not a crater in the sky nor a sinner on the streets
my first summoning was in St. John's Point
a narrow lane led me to a path, I passed an old man and
    some Pilgrims at midpoint
a few campers on the beach below and cows grazing at
    a standpoint.
The great discovery about the town itself
was a carpet factory and the links to South Africa
they made carpets for our Parliament, the White House
    and Dublin Castle
a humble little place in the heart of this town
with such a rich history and heritage.
Nestling between the valley and bog are two roads
one took me to Glencolmcille, an old Irish village on
    the left
the other to the Cliffs of Moher, a pilgrimage on the
    right
only by sheer chance I missed a turn on the way back
the wee road opened to the Trá where the sunset was an
    orange heft.
The chapel on the hill chimed me out of bed each
    morning with ringing bells

whilst seagulls lured me towards the big boats
a beautiful blue fish and chips cabin at the seafront
    awaits all day
for fishermen to unload their vessel to hungry onlookers
the old Irish tradition was that fish would be eaten every
    Friday.

PERPETUAL STAR
BRIAN LYNCH

Never to meet again
In the way they'd once done
And yet he had decided then
To be devoted in the old sense
Discovering lateness early
Unremedied and irremediable

Never to be really met again
Although remaining always in sight
Like the 'perpetual star' in the evening.

THE MORANDI BRIDGE
EILÉAN NÍ CHUILLEANÁIN

Let me lean my cheek against this limestone pillar –
I want to press until I feel the buzzing,
the sound the world makes when it isn't going
anywhere, a purr of grey transparent wings

hovering in one place. A humming to itself
because it needs to lie still, stay quiet and
recover, and who will help?
                              The noise
when the bridge fell down in Genova – the road

you and I drove along slowly, heading east
behind a small Fiat, packed and weighed down
with people, cake and flowers for a mother-in-law
that made a Sunday lunch; they were taking their time –

it was lunchtime again each year when we reached the
        bridge,
and the families were always on the move,
so we'd drive along slowly, those fifteen minutes
high up over the factories and streets –

I would tell you this news if the stones of the world
could carry language, but after eight months, the shock
And the noise inside them still, they cannot move
Or even allow a message to pass through.

From IN MEMORY OF EVA GORE-BOOTH AND CON MARKIEVICZ

W.B. YEATS

Dear shadows, now you know it all,
All the folly of a fight
With a common wrong or right.
The innocent and the beautiful
Have no enemy but time;
Arise and bid me strike a match
And strike another till time catch;
Should the conflagration climb,
Run till all the sages know.
We the great gazebo built,
They convicted us of guilt;
Bid me strike a match and blow.

BEGIN
BRENDAN KENNELLY

Begin again to the summoning birds
to the sight of the light at the window,
begin to the roar of morning traffic
all along Pembroke Road.
Every beginning is a promise
born in light and dying in dark
determination and exaltation of springtime
flowering the way to work.
Begin to the pageant of queuing girls
the arrogant loneliness of swans in the canal
bridges linking the past and future
old friends passing though with us still.
Begin to the loneliness that cannot end
since it perhaps is what makes us begin,
begin to wonder at unknown faces
at crying birds in the sudden rain
at branches stark in the willing sunlight
at seagulls foraging for bread
at couples sharing a sunny secret
alone together while making good.
Though we live in a world that dreams of ending
that always seems about to give in
something that will not acknowledge conclusion
insists that we forever begin.

Acknowledgements

The publishers gratefully acknowledge permission to reprint copyright material in this book as follows:

'A Blackthorn Winter' by Ann Leahy, reproduced with permission of the author.

'A Man from Derrybrien' by Patrick Deeley from *Groundswell: New and Selected* (Dedalus Press, 2013), reproduced with permission of Dedalus Press.

'After September' by Nicola Geddes from *Writing Home: The 'New Irish' Poets* (Dedalus Press, 2019), reproduced with permission of Dedalus Press.

'Against the Clock' by Derek Mahon from *Against the Clock* (The Gallery Press, 2018), reproduced with permission of the Author's Estate and The Gallery Press. www.gallerypress.com

'And Soul' by Eavan Boland from *New Selected Poems* (Carcanet, 2013), reproduced with permission of Carcanet Press.

'Begin' by Brendan Kennelly from *Familiar Strangers: New & Selected Poems 1960–2004* (Bloodaxe Books, 2004), reproduced with permission of Bloodaxe Books. www.bloodaxebooks.com

'blessing the boats' by Lucille Clifton from *How to Carry Water: Selected Poems of Lucille Clifton* (BOA Editions, 1991), reproduced with permission of The Permissions

Company, LLC on behalf of BOA Editions Ltd., www. boaeditions.org.

'Bull Island Haiku' by Pat Boran from *Waveforms* (Dedalus Press, 2015), reproduced with permission of Dedalus Press.

'Café' by Theo Dorgan from *Nine Bright Shiners* (Dedalus Press, 2014), reproduced with permission of Dedalus Press.

'Cyber You' by Julie O'Callaghan from *Magnum Mysterium* (Bloodaxe Books, 2020), reproduced with permission of Bloodaxe Books. www.bloodaxebooks.com

'Daidia'/'Daddy' by Caitlín Nic Íomhair, translated by Colette Bryce, from *Calling Cards* (The Gallery Press, 2018), reproduced with permission of the author, the translator and The Gallery Press. www.gallerypress.com

'Dán dom Athair'/'To My Father' by Michael Kirby from *Skelligs Haul* (Lilliput Press, 2019), reproduced with permission of Anne Coffey and The Lilliput Press.

'Do Not Ask: In Memory of Philip Casey, 4-2-2018' by Nessa O'Mahony from The Hollow Woman on the Island (Salmon Poetry), reproduced with permission of the author.

'Fás agus Bás'/'Growing and Dying' by Danny Sheehy, translated by Alan Titley, reproduced with permission of Máire Uí Shíthigh.

'Fear' by Ciaran Carson from *The Twelfth of Never* (The Gallery Press, 1998), reproduced with permission of the Author's Estate and The Gallery Press. www.gallerypress.com

'Home of Worship' by Abby Oliveira, reproduced with permission of the author.

'Lament' by Moya Cannon from *Keats Lives* (Carcanet, 2015), reproduced with permission of Carcanet Press.

'Late Fragment' by Raymond Carver from *A New Path to the Waterfall: Poems* (Atlantic Monthly Press, 1989), reproduced with permission of Grove Atlantic.

'Lives' by Gerard Smyth from *The Sundays of Eternity* (Dedalus Press, 2020), reproduced with permission of Dedalus Press.

'Ma' by Paul Muldoon from *New Selected Poems: 1968–1994* (Faber and Faber, 1996), reproduced with permission of Faber and Faber Ltd.

'Marbhna Oisín'/'Lament for Oisín' by Paddy Bushe from *Second Sight* (Dedalus Press, 2020), reproduced with permission of Dedalus Press.

'Matamaitic do shiansa ár n-anama' by Ceaití Ní Bheildiúin, reproduced with permission of the author.

'Memory of My Father' and 'In Memory of my Mother' by Patrick Kavanagh from *Collected Poems*, edited by Antoinette Quinn (Allen Lane, 2004), reproduced with permission of the Trustees of the Estate of the late Katherine B. Kavanagh, through the Jonathan Williams Literary Agency.

'Miracle' by Seamus Heaney from *Human Chain* (Faber and Faber, 2010), reproduced with permission of Faber and Faber Ltd.

Excerpt from 'Serenade' by Gerald Dawe from *Mickey Finn's Air* (The Gallery Press, 2014), reproduced with permission of the author and The Gallery Press. www.gallerypress.com

Excerpt from 'Spindrift' by Vona Groarke from *Spindrift* (The Gallery Press, 2009), reproduced with permission of the author and The Gallery Press. www.gallerypress.com

Excerpt from 'The Architect' by Jaki McCarrick from *Writing Home: The 'New Irish' Poets* (Dedalus Press, 2019), reproduced with permission of Dedalus Press.

Excerpt from 'The Keen for Art Ó Laoghaire' from *A Ghost in the Throat* by Doireann Ní Ghríofa (Tramp Press, 2020), reproduced with permission of the author.

Excerpt from *An Fear Dána* by Alan Titley (An Clóchomhar, 1993), reproduced with permission of the author.

Excerpt from *Nil Nil* by Don Paterson (Faber and Faber, 1993), reproduced with permission of Faber and Faber Ltd.

Haikus by Gabriel Rosenstock, reproduced with permission of the author.

Poets and translators

Akhmatova, Anna (1889–1966)

Boland, Eavan (1944–2020)

Bolger, Dermot (b. 1959)

Boran, Pat (b. 1963)

Bradstreet, Anne (b. 1612)

Bryce, Colette (b. 1970)

Bushe, Paddy (b. 1948)

Cannon, Moya (b. 1956)

Carson, Ciaran (1948–2019)

Carver, Raymond (1938–1988)

Clifton, Lucille (1936–2010)

Cullen, Catherine Ann (b. 1961)

Dhaliwal, Supriya Kaur

Dawe, Gerald (b. 1952)

Deeley, Patrick (b. 1953)

Dickinson, Emily (1830–1886)

Dorgan, Theo (b. 1953)

Duffy, Dorothy (b. 1959)

Dunne, Seán (1956–1995)

Ecclesiastes (450–200 BC)

Fallon, Peter (b. 1951)

Fiorentino, Viviana

French, Tom (b. 1966)

Geddes, Nicola (b. 1970)

Gleasure, James (b. 1940)

Glück, Louise (b. 1943)

Groarke, Vona (b. 1964)

Hardy, Thomas (1840–1928)

Heaney, Seamus (1939–2013)

Higgins, F.R. (1896–1941)

Higgins, Michael D. (b. 1941)

Kavanagh, Patrick (1904–1967)

Kennelly, Brendan (1936–2021)

Kirby, Michael (1906–2005)

Leahy, Ann (b. 1962)

Lynch, Brian (b. 1945)

Mac Aodha, Aifric (b. 1979)

Mahon, Derek (1941–2020)

McCarrick, Jaki

Meehan, Paula (b. 1955)

Mhac an tSaoi, Máire (1922–2021)

Montague, John (1929–2016)

Muldoon, Paul (b. 1951)

Ní Bheildiúin, Ceaití (b. 1958)

Ní Chleirchín, Caitríona (b. 1978)

Ní Chonaill, Eibhlín Dubh (1743–1800)

Ní Chuilleanáin, Eiléan (b. 1942)

Ní Dhomhnaill, Nuala (b. 1952)

Ní Ghríofa, Doireann (b. 1981)

Nic Íomhair, Caitlín (b. 1987)

Nistri, Giuliano (b. 1969)

Ó Cearbhalláin, Toirdhealbhach (1670–1738)

Ó Dálaigh, Muiríoch Albanach (c.1180–c.1250)

Ó Ríordáin, Seán (1916–1977)

O'Callaghan, Julie (b. 1954)

O'Donnell, John (b. 1960)

O'Driscoll, Dennis (1954–2012)

O'Leary, John (1953–2012)

Oliveira, Abby (b. 1982)

O'Mahony, Nessa (b. 1964)

O'Sullivan, Leanne (b. 1983)

Paterson, Don (b. 1963)

Rosenstock, Gabriel (b. 1949)

Russell, George William (AE) (1867–1935)

Sappho (630–570 BC)

Shakespeare, William (1564–1616)

Sheehy, Danny (1951–2017)

Shihab, Nye Naomi (b. 1952)

Smyth, Gerard (b. 1951)

Titley, Alan (b. 1947)

Tsugawa–Madden, Eriko (b. 1949)

Wheatley, David (b. 1970)

Whitman, Walt (1819-1892)

Williams, William Carlos (1883–1963)

Yeats, W.B. (1865–1939)

INDEX OF TITLES

INDEX OF FIRST LINES